HIT BY FRIENDLY FIRE

HIT BY FRIENDLY FIRE

What to do when fellow believers
hurt you

Michael A. Milton

 BOOKS

EP Books
Faverdale North, Darlington, DL3 0PH, England
e-mail: sales@epbooks.org
web: www.epbooks.org

133 North Hanover Street, Carlisle, PA 17013, USA.
e-mail: usasales@epbooks.org
web: www.epbooks.us

First published 2011

British Library Cataloguing in Publication Data available

ISBN 13 978 085234 776 8   ISBN 0 85234 776 6

Unless otherwise indicated, all Scripture quotations are from The
Holy Bible, English Standard Version, published by HarperCollins
Publishers © 2001 by Crossway Bibles, a division of Good News
Publishers. Used by permission. All rights reserved.

Printed and bound by Martins the Printers

Dedicated to
the Reverend and Mrs Robert E. Baxter and family,
who opened their hearts and home to a young family
seeking to follow Jesus Christ,
and showed us the way, through word and deed,
with love binding it all together;
and always to my wife, Mae.

And if one asks him, 'What are these wounds on your back?' he will say, 'The wounds I received in the house of my friends'
(Zechariah 13:6).

CONTENTS

Foreword

This book is designed to heal festering wounds, but healing is a painful process. It is the rule of the kingdom: to grow up, we must first grow *down* — in humility and authenticity; to receive a crown, we must first bear the cross.

Chances are, you chose this book because a friend has hurt you. But perhaps, though you may not wish to admit it, you have been the cause of the hurt. Either way, the path to peace and reconciliation is not an easy one. Actually, it is all too easy if we follow the Saviour's guidelines, but an Adamic trait in us makes the right path more difficult and less attractive.

My honest admission: I, too, have both hurt and been hurt by friends. Words, looks, gestures and jokes (the most hurtful weapons at our disposal) — all these I have used at some time or other. The memory of them still occasionally haunts me. Perhaps you know all too well what I mean. This book, then, is *for you.*

Allow me to make a confession in the interests of total disclosure. Mike Milton is both a dear friend and my boss. I am, therefore, somewhat prejudiced about what he writes. But this issue apart, I sincerely and enthusiastically endorse this book. Truth is, few people could write on this delicate subject with such authenticity and transparency. Just as we sometimes remark about a certain tie or shirt, 'It suits you,' so this theme suits Dr Milton. He is a man of conviction as well as warmth and passion. He is a leader who leads by example. His élan is infectious.

Books on forgiveness and reconciliation can sometimes produce more guilt than genuine help. The reason is often associated with a failure to see how the gospel works in the difficult issues of day-to-day relationships. I do so wish that Mike had written this book twenty years ago. It would have helped me, as it will now help you, in securing Christlike relationships in a broken and often fragile world. But had he written it then, it would not have been effused with so much grace and understanding.

It is now time for you to start reading and let a gentle and caring shepherd lead you with gospel grace and love to a place of peace and security. This is, after all, what the gospel of the grace that is in Jesus Christ is all about.

Derek W. H. Thomas

Minister for Preaching and Teaching,
First Presbyterian Church, Columbia,
Distinguished Visiting Professor of Systematic and
Historical Theology, RTS

PREFACE

It is now my aim, by the grace of God, to take a sermon which has been used of the Lord to touch many lives across the years, and to reshape it, expand the message and edit it for reading, so that more people around the world may realize, practically and really, what R. T. Kendall called *Total Forgiveness*.[1] There is great joy and freedom awaiting those in spiritual and mental bondage from being hurt by another Christian. These pages, and the prayers that follow each little chapter, are intended to be used by the reader for quiet meditation until, at last, the glorious power of new life and forgiveness and hope and resurrection transforms both the wounded and the one who wounds into cross-clinging, gospel-loving, quiet-spirited saints who esteem others higher than themselves, and who even glory in their trials for the sake of identifying with Christ.

My prayer is that the supernatural Word of God, a 'Word from another world', as my old professor, Dr Robert L. Reymond, Sr., called the Bible, will be redeployed from Scripture through these thoughts into the lives of many, for their good, for the glory of God and for the advancement of the gospel of Jesus Christ. Now, more than ever, in the old Christendom of the West, in the new Christendom of the global South and East and in the next Christendom that may be breaking forth in the Middle East — in other words, around the world, in all peoples and in all denominations — the church of our Lord Jesus Christ needs to be prepared for the spiritual warfare that the world, the flesh and the devil are waging with unprecedented intensity. Learning from Scripture how to deal with the wounds received in the house of a friend will be a foundational holy tactic for the church in this battle. May many souls be saved, others built up in the faith once delivered to the saints, and may there be wholeness in the Body of Christ!

Michael A. Milton

And it is always well for us to recollect the wounds of our Saviour. Often has he been wounded by professed friends, nay, even by his real disciples, when they act contrary to his word (Matthew Henry).

1.

HAVE YOU BEEN HURT BY ANOTHER BELIEVER?

One second. One mistake. One firing of the missile in the midst of the war. The missile cannot come back. The weapon is now headed for you. And the one who fired it is on your side. It is war. You have been hit by friendly fire.

And this is not Baghdad, or the Battle of the Bulge, or Pork Chop Hill. I am speaking of the many walking wounded in the body of Christ who have been hurt by other believers, people who have been hit by the betrayal of a Christian.

But this is no mistake. She meant to say those words. He meant to plot against you. They meant to bring you down. And you will never be the same. You will suffer with this for the rest of your life. You will not go back to any church. You will lick your wounds. You will be possessed by the pain for the rest of your life. And the pain becomes bitterness.

Do you know anyone like that? Or is that your story? Are you the victim of a wound inflicted by someone you love? Are you a victim?

It does not have to be. There is a way through the pain to know what to do when Christians hurt you. In order to find this answer, we must go to places in the Word of God which deal with the topic of pain. This subject, of betrayal within the house of those we love, is so common that one could diagnose the problem and seek the treatment from many different passages in the Bible. Yet I want to choose one example from the Old Testament and one from the New. One story involves Joseph. The other is about Paul. In each of these cases of being 'hit by friendly fire', I believe that the Lord will bring help and healing today.

Here is the inerrant and infallible Word where we will cast our anchor. Read it with a prayer, even now, for God to give you understanding and to send his Holy Spirit to hover over your heart until new life is brought out of the chaos that may be present there:

When Joseph's brothers saw that their father was dead, they said, 'It may be that Joseph will hate us and pay us back for all the evil that we did to him.' So they sent a message to Joseph, saying, 'Your father gave this command before he died, "Say to Joseph, Please forgive the transgression of your brothers and their sin, because they did evil to you." And now, please forgive the transgression of the servants of the God of your father.' Joseph wept when they spoke to him. His brothers also came and fell down before him and said, 'Behold, we are your servants.' But Joseph said to them, 'Do not fear, for am I in the place of God? As for you, you meant evil against me, but God meant it for good, to bring it about that many people should be kept alive, as they are today. So do not fear; I will provide for you and your little ones.' Thus he comforted them and spoke kindly to them (Genesis 50:15-21).

Some indeed preach Christ from envy and rivalry, but others from good will. The latter do it out of love, knowing that I am put here for the defence of the gospel. The former proclaim

Christ out of rivalry, not sincerely but thinking to afflict me in my imprisonment. What then? Only that in every way, whether in pretence or in truth, Christ is proclaimed, and in that I rejoice. Yes, and I will rejoice (Philippians 1:15-18).

Indeed, I count everything as loss because of the surpassing worth of knowing Christ Jesus my Lord. For his sake I have suffered the loss of all things and count them as rubbish, in order that I may gain Christ and be found in him, not having a righteousness of my own that comes from the law, but that which comes through faith in Christ, the righteousness from God that depends on faith — that I may know him and the power of his resurrection, and may share his sufferings, becoming like him in his death (Philippians 3:8-10).

Finally, I want to meditate upon the passage that I have chosen to summarize the theme of this little book:

And if one asks him, 'What are these wounds on your back?' he will say, 'The wounds I received in the house of my friends' (Zechariah 13:6).

Throughout this book, I will rely unflinchingly upon the truths of the person of Jesus Christ as the one who will bring healing. The arch principle of Peacemaker Ministries, which has had a profound impact on my own counselling of reconciliation, is a good foundation stone to place here:

> We believe that genuine peace between people can be found only through Jesus Christ. Therefore, we encourage people in conflict to believe the gospel and trust in Christ, and to faithfully rely on the promises and obey the commands that he has given to us in Scripture (see John 14:27; 2 Cor. 5:18-19; Col. 3:15-16; 2 Tim. 3:16).'[1]

Now begin a time of opening your heart to the Word of the Lord. What I am going to unfold in the following pages will quite possibly startle some of you. But if you are startled by God's Word into finding the new life, then the angels will rejoice. And the church of Jesus Christ will be stronger in our generation.

A prayer

O Father of light, shine forth the light of your love, even the love of Christ Jesus your Son, my Lord, so that I can see the truth of your Word and be able, through the Holy Spirit, to apply this word to my life. I long for healing. I long for the touch of the Master on my fevered brow. Come, Lord Jesus, in your Word and open my soul to receive the nourishment I need from you. I now come before you as I enter upon this study to reveal the wounds, to name them and to admit that without your power I am destined to be among the walking wounded in the church; but with your power I have hope for healing, hope for a new life and a new level of service to God and man. In the hope of the gospel I pray. Amen.

After conversion we need bruising so that reeds
may know themselves to be reeds, not oaks
(Richard Sibbes).[1]

2.
INTERRUPTED BY GOD

I do sermon planning, and then I do sermon preparation. In sermon planning, I establish a period of time, such as a year, and seek the Lord to take us through books or chapters of the Bible. Then, week-to-week, I do sermon preparation — based upon the planning — where I actually prepare for the next sermon coming up. Between series on books or chapters, I bring single-sermon messages. In this way, I generally know where I am going. However, in some cases, between the planning and the preparation, God interrupts my life.

And that is the way it should be.

So I believe this message has come from the Lord. I would characterize this little book as pastoral counselling for the Body of Christ, drawn from Scripture, to

address a common spiritual disease that I have wit-
nessed over the years and among many Christians. I see
this as a universal need in the lives of Christians — and,
I must say, in the lives of non-Christians. It is the matter
of being hurt by one you love. It is the matter of seeing
yourself as a victim — or not — in that process. Let me
tell you how God brought this to me, and then I want to
address it from God's Word.

Some years ago, as I was reviewing my schedule for
that particular day, I noticed that I had three appointments with three different families. None of the families
were from my congregation, or even from my city, for
that matter. As a matter of fact, each of them was
involved in full-time gospel ministry in one way or
another.

During the first appointment, the family began to
share their story. But soon the words, going nowhere as
far as I could tell, ended in tears. Then they said it: 'We
have been hurt by other Christians.' I spent no small
amount of time with them. I brought them to God's
Word, and we sought the truths of Scripture. Our time
was over.

Then I came to the second appointment and the
second family. This husband and wife began to relate

various details within a larger rambling narrative that became more complex as they told it. I slowed them down and attempted to help them identify the heart-ache within the story. It was not hard to find: 'We have been betrayed by another believer in our ministry. We feel as if we cannot go on. The pain is so deep it is affecting our entire lives.'

I was amazed: two appointments and two identical issues. However, my astonishment over the similarity of these stories would not be complete.

Time for the third appointment: I was almost ready to say, 'All right, so how were *you* hurt by another believer?' But the man shared his concern about a vocational decision. He told me that he was considering another call to ministry. I prayed, 'All right, Lord. Great! This is not a trend.' We spoke about the man's vo-cational crisis — seeking God's will on what to do with his life. Finally, holding back tears, he interrupted our flow of conversation with the real issue behind his story of vocational change: 'Pastor, I am in this dilemma because another Christian hurt me! I am having to leave the field and find another ministry because of being hurt by another believer!' Tears welled up in his eyes — and mine as well. I was overcome by the tsunami of pain devastating the Body of Christ. Are we seemingly devouring each other? I cried out, 'Lord, isn't it enough that the devil, the flesh and the world are after us? Must we also turn against ourselves?'

Over the years of gospel ministry, both as pastor of a local church and now serving a seminary, I have seen these scenarios repeat themselves time and time again. I suspect that eight out of ten Christians reading these words have been hurt by someone they love or respect. I base my observations not only upon my experience, but also upon the stories that other pastors and church leaders have shared with me. Is there a pastor reading this booklet who is no longer in a pulpit because a toxic parishioner has hurt him? Whenever I address missionaries or pastors, and especially pastor's wives and children, I know that these kinds of wounds are present. Are you a lay leader who has been hurt by a manipulative pastor, or by a fellow leader in the church or ministry? The problem is by no means limited to any one tradition within the Christian church. It is not limited to laity or clergy, to Western or Eastern churches. No, it is clear that betrayal is universal.

I call this 'friendly fire'. It is the flak that we take from our own side. It is the misguided missile that is laser-guided by a twisted pathology of the human soul, still under sanctification, still seeking, in the best cases, to mortify the residue of sin that remains from an old life away from Christ, which hits and explodes on impact in our hearts. It could also be described as being 'wounded in the house of a friend'. This is what Zechariah calls it:

> And if one asks him, 'What are these wounds on your back?' he will say, 'The wounds I received in the house of my friends' (Zechariah 13:6).

Zechariah spoke of being 'wounded in the house of … friends'. What did he mean? While we look first to the Old Testament context to see that the prophet understood that faithful witness to God created retribution and consequent wounds from those of his own people who assailed him out of a supposed zeal to please God, we must agree with the many believing commentators who assert that the text also points to our Lord Jesus Christ. It is imperative that we see this, as Jamieson, Fausset and Brown commented:

> The Holy Spirit in Zechariah alludes indirectly to Messiah, the Antitype, wounded by those

whom He came to befriend, who ought to have
been His 'friends', who were His kinsmen.[2]

Our Lord Jesus Christ, indeed, knew the pain of
being wounded in the house of his friends:

> He who ate my bread has lifted his heel
> against me (John 13:18).
>
> He came to his own, and his own people did
> not receive him (John 1:11).

As we examine the Word of God on this subject, we
discover that betrayal in the house of our own friends,
our own people, is, sadly, mysteriously, all too common
in the record of God's people. From the patriarchs to
Moses, from David to the prophets, and even to our
Lord, the cycle of 'friendly fire' and the resulting deep,
often lifelong, emotional pain and spiritual scarring
from others of our own household, or from those in our
own church, repeats itself.

Why do we hurt each other? Another book could be
written on that topic alone. But briefly, as a pastor, let
me summarize what I have observed. We hurt each
other for many reasons, often intertwined: we have been
hurt, so we 'desire' to hurt others so that others can

share our pain; we are honestly insensitive to the feelings of others because we have experienced God in a certain way and have unrealistic expectations that others will share the same experience that we did (and if they don't, we question whether their faith is genuine). We hurt each other when, through neglect of our own souls, or besetting sins that are not unveiled to the light of the gospel in confession, we have allowed roots of bitterness to grow.

Each of these reasons points to a failure to be fashioned by the Word of God. Sanctification, which is this growth in grace and knowledge of Christ that leads to virtue in the Christian life, is snuffed out by the world, the flesh and the devil as we fail to drink from the fountain of grace through Word, sacrament and prayer. Without drinking from the divine draught of Christ's very person, we become dry and graceless in our souls, and therefore we have no reserves to draw upon when conflict arises.

We may have a personality flaw that developed from childhood. We go about saying, 'That's just the way I am,' and expect that others, and God, will tolerate it as just a 'personality flaw' that is a 'take it or leave it' proposition. How sinful, yet how real this is! Some of us manipulate others because we honestly don't know how else to communicate. Virtues of honest, clean, godly communication have never been modelled for us in our homes of origin. We are 'clueless' as to how to get along with others in a community of believers, where misunderstandings, sin-infested words and plain old stupid decisions are the norm.

All of these causes have their root in original sin, or in the influence of the world, or in the activity of the devil who goes about like a roaring lion, seeking whom he may devour (and the church is filled with 'red meat' for Satan to go after). But, more tellingly, we hurt each other because the motif of the cross includes betrayal — patterned after the betrayal of our Lord — and since he said that the disciple is not above his Master, we should expect the same treatment. However painful and dysfunctional this may seem, it is a present reality until we are all perfected in glorification. The question is: what do you do about it? Or, to make it personal, will you remain a victim, or will you move to being a victor with Christ?

A prayer

Lord God, who gave your only begotten Son that he might live the life I cannot live, and die an atoning death for my sins, rekindle within me a desire to begin this spiritual journey with an investigation into my own soul. Lord, I read these words and realize that I too have leaned too long on excuses for my behaviour. I am dry and need the moisture of the grace and love of Christ to renew my spirit. Come, Lord Jesus, even now, and show me my sin and my need of the gospel of Christ in my daily walk with you. I offer this prayer in Jesus' name.

Hence proceed those spiritual desertions in which he often leaves us to ourselves, in regard to both grace and comfort, that we may know the spring-head of these to be outside ourselves. Hence it is that in the mount, that is, in extremities, God is the most seen (Richard Sibbes).[1]

3.
WHEN THE CLOCK STOPS

I once sold insurance door-to-door in low-income areas of Louisiana. One of my clients was a poor family who lived in an old house in a run-down part of town. Every month I would personally meet them in their home to collect their insurance money. Afterwards, we would sit in their living room and talk. One day I noticed that the clock was wrong. It said nine o'clock when, in fact, it was noon. I said nothing. But I saw the same thing the next month, and then the following. Finally, I mentioned something to the husband and wife. Tears came to their eyes. 'That was the moment our boy died ten years ago,' the husband whispered as he held his sobbing wife. I looked away at the clock once again, and understood. The clock had stopped in their lives at the moment they lost their boy.

The pain of friendly fire can stop the clock. When wounded by a friend in our own house, it is hard to go on. There is no pain like it. This happens to Christians who are hurt by other Christians and who fail to identify their pain with Christ. The clock stops. They go through life, month after month, year after year, and often church after church, but in many cases the clock stopped in their lives years ago, when they were hurt. In some sense one could even say that part of their faith died at that time. They were disillusioned. They were heartbroken. They would never be the same again.

Yet, I wonder, how many reading these words are living their lives with the 'clock stopped'?

Today victimhood seems to be an accepted way of living. As a minister of the gospel, I see walking-wounded victims of abuse, of scandal, of failed marriages and of unhappy childhoods. As a minister of the gospel I can also feel a sense of being wounded, a tendency towards victimhood, in my own being. It is part of the fallen condition of our humanity.

However, living as a victim is not living at all, because life cannot go forward when the clock has stopped at the point of our last betrayal. God did not intend that you should live as a victim. That is not the gospel way. Victimhood in the body of Christ may be normal (for who goes through life without some chinks in our armour, to one degree or another?), but taking on the identity of a victim and living like that for years is not the gospel way. Now, I do not propose a moralistic answer that just says, 'Shape up; stiff upper lip. Chop, chop. Get up and get on with it.' Neither is that sort of unbiblical Stoicism which denies the human pain that we all may feel a pathway to healing; but, rather, it is a formula for a more complicated disease of the soul.

There is another way: the gospel way, the way of the cross, which will lead to deep healing for this abysmal lesion in the Body of Christ, the church. But I warn you, it will involve another kind of pain — the pain of Christ's cross. However, Christ's cross will bring resurrection, and the new life he brings will also make the clock start ticking again.

In the gospel story, revealed over time from Joseph through Paul and down to your life and mine, the person or situation that seeks to destroy us becomes a channel through which the hands of a sovereign and loving God can reach to save us. This is the gospel. This is the preaching of the cross, where the 'emblem of suffering and shame' became the sacred sign of victory and new life. Embracing this pattern of living, admittedly *contra mundum* — against the wisdom of this world — leads from victimhood to victory. But it is not an easy road. It is, however, the only road to healing.

Turning to our chosen Old Testament passage, this is what we perceive in Joseph's capacity to forgive his brothers after they literally 'ditched' him (and Joseph's boastful preaching about his dream of superiority over his brothers is understood to be connected to this retribution, however unjust). Wisely, Joseph identified his pain with God. In God's purposes, the pain was intended to bring about a blessing. Being hurt by his brothers made sense. The pain of false accusation made sense. The trial of unjust imprisonment was good. The years of separation from his father were good for him. He was saying with Moses:

> Make us glad for as many days as you have af-
> flicted us,
> and for as many years as we have seen evil
>   (Psalm 90:15).

The power at work in the life of Joseph is what you need in order to get past this hurt. It is the power that was present in Paul when he said in Galatians 2:

> I have been crucified with Christ. It is no longer I who live, but Christ who lives in me. And the life I now live in the flesh I live by faith in the Son of God, who loved me and gave himself for me (Galatians 2:20).

In our text from Philippians, Paul embraces the pain that comes at him, and in so doing identifies with Jesus Christ. This allows Paul to move from being victim to victor.

Isn't that what you want for your life? Isn't that what you desire for your church, which today, as you read this, may be fractured from the pain of infighting and rips and tears in the bridal gown of the church? There is hope here in God's Word, and there is healing for the walking wounded.

What I shared with those three families that I met with years ago is the same message that I want to share with you today as though I were your pastor. For believers hurt by other believers, for loved ones hurt by other loved ones, for anyone feeling like a victim of another person, or maybe just feeling betrayed by life, you can move from being victim to victor and deal with the pain of betrayal or suffering by taking three severe steps.

We see these steps being taken by Paul, who is in prison as a result of the plotting of his own people (Philippians 3:10-11) and by Joseph, who was mistreated by his own brothers (Genesis 50:19-20).

We also see the goal before us who are the wounded:

> That I may know him and the power of his resurrection, and may share his sufferings, becoming like him in his death, that by any means possible I may attain the resurrection from the dead (Philippians 3:10-11).

Let us now begin our journey to explore these crucial steps that the Holy Spirit will show us.

A prayer

O my Father, the Father of our Lord Jesus Christ, who knew loneliness and betrayal and heartache on the cross, teach me to bring my questions to you. Help me now to sit at your feet and learn the way of peace. Help me to appropriate the gospel of your grace to my life. Help me to demonstrate that gospel in my dealings with others, even those who have hurt me. I ask it for the cause of Christ and the good of the generations who will follow me until you come again. In Jesus' name. Amen.

I have been crucified with Christ and I no longer live, but Christ lives in me. The life I live in the body, I live by faith in the Son of God, who loved me and gave himself for me
(Galatians 2:20, NIV).

4.
TAKE UP YOUR CROSS

St Paul, imprisoned in Rome, being used by — of all
people — other preachers, suffered the indignity of
isolation and shame. This is the sad scenario that the
apostle describes in the first chapter of the Epistle to the
Philippians:

> Some indeed preach Christ from envy and
> rivalry, but others from good will. The latter do it
> out of love, knowing that I am put here for the
> defence of the gospel. The former proclaim
> Christ out of rivalry, not sincerely but thinking to
> afflict me in my imprisonment (Philippians
> 1:15-17).

Yet Paul, who could have claimed victimhood if ever anyone could have, answered that scenario, not with Stoicism, but rather with a faith born out of a spirit that was out of this world. Read his response to being mistreated by other believers:

> What then? Only that in every way, whether in pretence or in truth, Christ is proclaimed, and in that I rejoice. Yes, and I will rejoice (Philippians 1:18).

How could this misused minister have the capacity to say that truthfully? The answer is that Paul preached the gospel to his own soul and identified his life with that of the central motif of the cross of Christ. Read and meditate on his words later in the epistle: '... that I may know him and the power of his resurrection, and may share his sufferings, becoming like him in his death' (Philippians 3:10).

This is difficult language. It is especially difficult if you are approaching the test as one who has been hurt by others. What can it possibly mean for you? Well, surely Paul cannot go again to the cross to atone for his sins. That is not what he means. What Paul means to say is that every sorrow, every act of treachery, every act of betrayal has become, for him, a point of identification with Christ. Through these hits by other believers, he not only knows the cross and entombment in that cell, but he knows resurrection as well.

Paul is given a cross. His cross is imprisonment. The imprisonment is because of betrayal and treachery on the part of people who should have loved him and encouraged him. In Philippians 1 it is the betrayal and treachery of fellow preachers of the gospel. In Philippians 3 it is the betrayal and treachery and plotting of the Jews. In so many ways we see this man betrayed, and he is now in prison. But Paul will say, 'I want you to know, brothers, that what has happened to me has really served to advance the gospel' (Philippians 1:12).

Then, after talking about the betrayal and the rivalry of ministry, Paul says that whether Christ is preached in pretence or in truth, he is preached. That is enough for the apostle, and he rejoices.

How do you move from being hurt to rejoicing? The answer is: 'You take up your cross.' That is not an easy answer, but it is necessary. As Anglican Archbishop Henry Luke Orombi of Uganda once told me, 'So much of our response in the Christian life could be summarized as *difficult but necessary*.'[1] So it is with our response to being hit by friendly fire — it is difficult but necessary.

This is what Christ commanded us to do when he said that we must take up our cross:

> Then Jesus told his disciples, 'If anyone would come after me, let him deny himself and take up his cross and follow me. For whoever would save his life will lose it, but whoever loses his life for my sake will find it' (Matthew 16:24-25; see also Mark 8:34; Luke 9:23-24).

The person who is hurt, and who is not moving on to embrace that pain as a means for God to do something in his life, is the person who is stuck and for whom the clock has stopped. Why? The reason is that he is not denying himself. In fact, the very thing he wants to do is to feed self — '... my rights; they hurt me; they should do this; they said this about me; I need to be justified; I need to be taken care of; I was offended.' But Jesus says, 'Take up your cross; follow me; deny yourself; whoever seeks to save his life will lose it; whoever loses his life for my sake will find it.'

We want to think about cross-bearing as physical pain, and it is. We want to think about taking up our cross as standing up for truth and maybe taking some hits for the sake of it, perhaps even being a martyr for it. Throughout church history many have done so. But the context of the cross is also betrayal. The context of the cross is the pain of being hurt by those close to us.

Zechariah 13:6 speaks of 'the wounds I received in the house of my friends'. This is the painful life that the people who came to my office were speaking of. This is the pain you may feel in your heart. This may be where some of you are living today.

Sadly, some people live by the words of the late American playwright, Tennessee Williams, who opined: 'We have to distrust each other. It is our only defence against betrayal.'[2] This is wrong. God does not call us to live in distrust, but to live in faith in Christ. It is not that I implicitly trust all men; it is that I trust God in all situations. And this makes life sweet.

Recently, I was told about a friend from my past who had moved. I asked where he was going to church and was told that he goes nowhere. He speaks of past betrayals, past pain in churches, and says that he will not allow himself to be hurt again. He distrusts. This is now his defence against betrayal. His philosophy of life was related to me by his ten-year-old son. What a lesson that boy is getting, for his father's pain is infecting his life as well!

God has revealed that he does not desire that we should live with a legacy of bitterness. Rather, the lesson is that you and I are called to take up our cross in every way, including our relationships. It is true that you may be hurt. But you are a disciple of one who was betrayed, who was hurt, and you are no better than Jesus.

To follow Christ is to embrace the cross, to say with the Bible, 'Although he was a son, he learned obedience through what he suffered' (Hebrews 5:8). We are not gluttons for punishment. We are not masochistic and do not desire pain. We are followers of Christ and, to identify with Christ, we bring all of our heartache to him. We find meaning in our suffering, even in our betrayals, through Christ.

In dealing with the experience of being hurt by others, to take up the cross is to stop being a victim and to begin to be a victor through Jesus Christ.

Think about what God is teaching victims in Genesis 50:

> But Joseph said to them, 'Do not fear, for am I in the place of God? As for you, you meant evil against me, but God meant it for good, to bring it

about that many people should be kept alive, as they are today' (Genesis 50:19-20).

In my own life, I have sought to be reminded of this through a phrase from a Puritan prayer that I have written down in my devotional notebook. When I fill up one journal and purchase another, I always go to the front and write down these words: 'Give me perpetual broken-heartedness; keep me always clinging to thy cross.' This plea feeds my soul each day and helps me to remember to identify with the cross, and even to desire the brokenness that comes from it (that I may take my burden to Christ and thereby know him all the more).

To live thus, with this way of gospel thinking, requires drinking plenty of grace from the fountains that deliver the refreshing streams of the life of Christ Jesus. It also requires time spent with God in his Word and in prayer and in the company of his people in worship.

So this is your starting point for responding to the friendly fire and to being hurt by other believers.

Now we can identify our second step. If the first step in moving from being victim to victor in our painful relationships is to take up our cross, the second is also to follow Christ in the gospel pattern that leads to healing.

A prayer

O Father, your Son, who took up his cross, though he despised it, did so for our salvation. Lord, you taught us to take up our crosses and follow you. Yet we are so often fearful of crosses. Show us that the way up is down. Lead us to assume trials with joy, as James teaches us. This is supernatural, Lord. We cannot do it without your divine power. So we wait upon you, Lord, with great expectation. We lift this prayer to you, O God, in the name of your Son, our Saviour, Jesus Christ.

God not only permits sinful acts, but he directs
and controls them to the determination of his
own purposes
(A. A. Hodge).[1]

5.
TAKE OFF YOUR CROWN

Stop pretending you are sovereign and confess the truth that only God is sovereign. J. C. Ryle wrote, 'Of all the doctrines of the Bible, none is so offensive to human nature as the doctrine of God's sovereignty.'[2]

I have found this to be true in my nature. It is the final act of submission — to say that I am not in control, but God is. In confessing this, you will find healing.

If you are in control, then your crucifixion has no meaning. You must hold hostage in your heart that person who is perpetrating this injustice upon you. You cannot forgive because you have been wronged.

But if God is sovereign, then the one who brought your cross is Christ himself. This is hard language. It means that like Joseph, like Paul — and, yes, most like

Jesus — you see God sovereignly ruling in all of life to bring you to the point of crucifixion. Crucifixion is, as Gene Edwards puts it in his book *Crucified by Christians*,[3] meant to destroy. God has destruction on his mind in your life. He intends to purge, to refine. As the old Puritan Thomas Watson put it, his purpose is to put the gold into the fire until the last dross has drained from the metal. Jesus was crucified by his Father. And it was to his Father that he cried.

In my counselling sessions with the three families mentioned earlier, things became very still — even uncomfortable — at this point. Maybe it is so with you right now. But Joseph escaped being a victim and became a victor by naming God, not as the author of evil, but as the one who caused it to work together for good. Paul was not bitter against the Jews. He would pray for them, would say that he was prepared to give his life for them, even though they had betrayed him and he would suffer and ultimately lose his life because of their condemnation against him. Why? Because God was in control of Paul's crucifixion. God, not man, is in control of our tribulations, our 'crucifixions' if you will.

Reflect on the way Matthew Henry summed up the fact of the sovereignty of God and the painful — and even sinful — things that are sent to us:

> God often brings good out of evil, and pro-motes the designs of his providence even by the sins of men; not that he is the author of sin, far be it from us to think so; but his infinite wisdom so overrules events that ... the issue, that ends in his praise [was at first]... to his dishonour; as [in] the putting of Christ to death.[4]

We need the courage from God to say with Jonathan Edwards, 'Absolute sovereignty is what I love to ascribe to God... It has often been my delight.'[5]

During a conference I attended recently, I listened intently to a well-known pastor of a large American Presbyterian congregation. The minister, addressing other pastors, spoke with great transparency about his struggles with applying God's sovereignty to his own life. He said that there was a time when his wife grew tired of his supposed sense of control and put a sticky note on the bathroom mirror that read, 'When will you stop trying to be the general manager of the world?'

Ouch! Any 'general managers of the world' out there? As one recovering controller to another, you know there is only one. And that is good news. Because the crucial step in coming to terms with any pain that has come against us, including being hurt by someone close to us, is to say, 'God, you are in control. What do you want me to learn?' This releases people to let God deal with them. It focuses your pain, not on someone who hurt you, but on the God who has led you to your own Calvary. Or, as Malcolm Muggeridge once put it, 'Every happening, great and small, is a parable whereby God speaks to us, and the art of life is to get the message.'[6]

Years ago I heard Dr D. James Kennedy preach on the doctrine of God's sovereignty. I was a young man at the time, who had been hurt by a childhood as an orphan, through abuse and through a host of other things — many of them involving 'believers' who hurt me. When Dr Kennedy preached of a God who 'turned it to gold',[7] it changed my life. The doctrine of God's sovereignty became the balm that led me to praise Jesus as the Lord of my life. His sovereign reign over all things, even the hurtful things, brought me closer to him. I have learned that without the pain I would not have gone to him in prayer. Without the prayer there would have been no healing. Without the healing there would be no abundance of eternal life. Thus, in a strange, upside-down, gospel way, I can 'bless' the circumstances of life, even the evil actions of others who sought to hurt me, as being the resources of this loving, sovereign God who used all things to bring me to him! It can be so in your life.

I wrote a song, the first song I wrote after I understood this truth that set me free, called 'He's in Control'. Here are the words that might, perhaps, be of encouragement to you too.

Of all of the things I've been told,
there's none that more thrills my soul
than knowing that God's in control;
it gives me the strength to go on.

Whether it's good or it's bad,
no reason for me to be sad;
God's given us all that he had,
when he gave up his only Son.

He's in control; he's in control,
tenderly sculpting my soul

> to the image of Christ my King;
> he's in control.

There was a time when I thought,
life was a chance to be bought,
but I was confused and distraught
by the lies that I'd been told,

So God in his mercy and might,
allowed me to see the light,
and I know now that it's all alright,
I know who is in control.

In the darkest night of your soul,
when the storms of life begin to blow,
you can rest your head on this soft pillow,
and you can know...

> He's in control, he's in control,
> tenderly crafting your soul
> to the image of Christ your King;
> he's in control.[8]

Grasping God's sovereignty — not as a theological concept, but as an act of utter submission and childlike faith — will move you from the status of a victim to a victor.

We have worked through two steps: first, take it to the cross; second, take off your crown. But it all comes together with the third step.

A prayer

O Father, we confess that so often we have not followed our Lord Jesus Christ, who left his royal robes of heaven to assume the flesh of man and the person of a servant. Help us to yield our hearts and minds to your sovereign grace. Help us to trust you in that sovereign grace that we may be free in Christ. In Jesus' name I pray. Amen.

It is for the lack of this subordination that we so often miss the guidance we seek. There is a secret controversy between our will and God's. And we shall never be right till we have let him take, and break, and make. Oh, do seek for that! If you cannot give, let him take. If you are not willing, confess that you are willing to be made willing. Hand yourself over to him to work in you, to will and to do of his own good pleasure. We must be as plastic clay, ready to take any shape that the great Potter may choose, so shall we be able to detect his guidance

(F. B. Meyer).[1]

6.
Go to your Gethsemane

Paul writes that he wants to identify his sufferings with Christ so 'that by any means possible I may attain the resurrection from the dead' (Philippians 3:11). This was a crucial step in Paul's understanding of God's will in his life. The apostle recognized (recognition of God's providence comes with walking with God over the years and observing his ways) that God guided him to the Roman prison through the sins of brethren, in order to cause Paul to know Christ's resurrection (and this, we are told, was working towards strengthening the faith of the saints as well as advancing the gospel to the highest echelons of the Roman Empire).

Deciding that his brothers' awful act of treachery was under the sovereign control of God was a moment of release of a powerful faith for Joseph. Thus, for both Paul and Joseph, recognizing God's sovereignty brought about spiritual freedom, the ability to forgive and to release events and people into the hands of God. It was — and when we follow this pattern, it is — the way we stop playing God and 'allow' God to be as original in bringing healing to others' lives as he was in our own.

Gethsemane is the place where, like Jesus, like Paul and like Joseph, you come face to face with your crucifixion and with the fact that God is in control. Note carefully: if there is to be resurrection — a new life to emerge from the pain, the betrayal, the hurtful words — there must be a crucifixion; and if there is to be a crucifixion — by the Father for the good of many — then there must be a Gethsemane moment when you say, 'Not my will but yours.' There must be a moment when you say, even when the shadow of pain is falling over you, 'They meant it for evil, but God meant it for good.'

This Gethsemane — your Gethsemane, the moment when you respond to the pain you received from others — is the turning point when you will either go forward as one of the walking wounded, destined to carry the burden for years, or you will accept the trial as coming from God and open your life to him. If you take up your cross and take off your crown, your response of faith will lead you to trust totally in the Lord and in his will for your life, which in turn means total forgiveness of others and release of them to the Lord for his will in their lives, and total freedom for you and his wonderful grace being unleashed as a powerful reality.

This is what I shared with the friends whom I counselled that day. And it is what I want to say to each of you, because we shall all be hurt. We are all a bunch of recovering sinners living with each other. Like a family, we say things that hurt; we make mistakes that hurt others and ourselves. We live in a world that is fallen and where we are always being victimized by someone or something. But the Lord is calling us to identify our sufferings with Christ so that we are becoming like him through the things that come against us.

I want to share something with you. I don't say it to bring attention to myself, but to show God's faithfulness. There was a time in my ministry when some things came together to bring pain. I cannot tell you details about these times, for they are too painful to me and too personal for others. But I did not see this truth. As I was hurt, I brooded over my pain. I believe that I was unforgiving in my heart towards these people, and towards one man in particular. The pain festered for a

long time. I would say, 'This man has hurt me and
ruined something good for me.' I hope that by now you
see I was wrong. There is no resurrection for those who
suffer without Gethsemane submission. There is no new
life. There is only the grave. But if that is your story, it
does not have to end that way. There is always a Gethsemane moment available for you. For me, I found my
Gethsemane in a hotel room when no one else was
watching. I said, 'Lord, you did this. Not that man. Not
those people. You did this. And shall I not drink this
cup?' I had lost much. I cried and I cried. The tomb
opened. I rose, and I lived again.

One day, many years later, I again saw the shadow of
a cross coming over me. This time, I remembered. I am
sorry, but again I cannot tell you details. However, I will
tell you this: I came home to my wife and said, 'The
Lord has called us to the field of testing. We have
entered the time of the cross.' The crucifixion came. I
felt moments when the Father had abandoned me. But
by then I knew that he had abandoned his Son, my Lord,
so that he would never abandon me. I knew from my
lesson in the cross that to embrace the situation that
brought pain would mean release and forgiveness
towards those who may have seemed to bring the

hammer and the nails and the cross. No, it was God who would do this. For, as one writer put it:

> Love...
> ordains every struggle to strengthen us,
> lights every furnace to purify us,
> mingles every bitter cup to heal us.[2]

I have never known God's love more than when I took up the cross, took off the crown and went to my own Gethsemane.

I shared this testimony with these three families, and I saw God moving to bring new life. It didn't take years of counselling. It took one moment of saying, 'I want to know him and the power of his resurrection in my life. I want to take up my cross and follow him, to claim him as sovereign King, even in my rejection and my betrayals.' I watched faces lift up from prayers of confession to joyful release, years of pent-up pain dripping away and new life, like fresh sunshine, coming through.

God will do it for you, too. He will transform you, who have been hurt, wounded, abandoned, sinned against, betrayed, from a victim to a victor by trusting in the one who was hurt, wounded, abandoned, sinned against and betrayed, but who pronounced forgiveness from the cross. Jesus Christ has transformed the cross from an instrument of destruction sent by the Father to an instrument of salvation ordained by God. In him there can be no more victims — only victors.

How many who are reading this will now pause and pray, 'I want to know him and the power of his resurrection, and share in his sufferings, becoming like him in his death, that by any means possible I may rise again'?

How many will believe that they meant it for evil, but God meant it for good? To go to Gethsemane is to go into the quiet place of giving up your rights, your will, your privilege, to Jesus.

The garden sanctuary awaits you now.

A prayer

O Lord God, I am ready to fall down before you in this very moment. I ask that you cause this time to become my 'Gethsemane' before you. I want to do your will. I want to surrender my will to yours. I do not understand why I have been hurt. I don't understand fully why I had to suffer. But I know that in doing so I may identify with Christ Jesus my Lord, who suffered infinitely more than I have ever done. Draw me, therefore, with your Spirit closer to you and to the very wounds of Jesus my Lord, in whose name I pray. Amen.

Faith is defined in Scripture as 'the assurance of things hoped for, the conviction of things not seen' (Heb. 11:1)... Do you put your full trust in God despite what you see happening around you? Do you rejoice in him regardless of your circumstances?

(John Currid).[1]

7.
DON'T GIVE UP ON THE CHURCH

Joseph came to understand, by faith, that God was in control of his circumstances, and he didn't give up on his family. Likewise, Paul recognized the sinful activity of his brother preachers who were gloating over his imprisonment as they seethed in their vocational jealousy. Yet Paul did not give up on them. Paul believed that, whether in pretence or not, the gospel was being preached. Christ looked down from Calvary and forgave those who were crucifying him. He was able to see that this most heinous of cosmic crimes was being used by God to redeem a world of sinners.

God is in control in all things and is causing his church to go forward, even in the midst of our broken conditions. If we don't get this right, if we fail to understand that betrayal and misunderstanding and painful actions happen in the house of friends, we shall become disillusioned with the church, if not with God himself. This almost happened to me. Let me share my story.

Soon after my wife and I committed our lives to the God of grace and the sovereign Lord who was much bigger than we ever imagined, we began attending a new congregation.[2] The pastor preached God's sovereignty and God's grace and, as far as we could see, the Spirit was moving powerfully in the midst of this congregation. We were wide-eyed and perhaps just a little idealistic and unrealistic in our expectations of the church on this side of glory. We assumed that, since we were all depending on God's grace, we would just 'naturally' all get along. You can see that our theology of sanctification was obviously limited!

The church exists in the tension between the people we are and the people we are called to be. That tension is increasingly, practically, addressed by the ministry of the Lord shaping us through the means of grace throughout the whole of our lives. I did not possess that mature theology then, and the resulting situation led to tremendous pain. For little did I know that there was a split brewing in the congregation (over who knows what; I cannot remember even now, which is usually the case in such matters).

I discovered this raw nerve threatening the life of the congregation one winter night at a 'fellowship' supper. As many of us were standing about talking and laughing and balancing hot drinks in polystyrene cups in one hand, and overloaded dessert samplings on flimsy paper plates in the other, I decided to introduce myself to several people I didn't know. I put down my cup and shook the hand of the gentleman closest to me, gave a smiling greeting to the lady next to him and made my way around the room like that. As I approached one professional-looking fellow, an officer in the church as I recall, I noticed that he was looking at me with some concern. 'He is wondering who the new fellow around here is, I guess,' I thought to myself. Well, as I came up to him, I put down the cup, and reached out my hand to shake his.

I will never forget what happened next. This brother in the Lord, as I took him to be, looked down at my outstretched hand, then looked up and stared at me with obvious anger and said, 'No thanks! You've chosen your side by speaking with —. If you are on that side, you are not on mine!' His moustache-covered mouth down-turned, and his face red with obvious fury, he spun around on his heels and left the room.

I was devastated. What had I done? It became immediately apparent that he was upset with me because I had talked with someone else in the room whom he considered to be 'on the other side' of the split. Through my ignorance of the situation, I had inadvertently 'chosen' sides by conversing happily with his 'enemies'. I remember putting all of those pieces together in my mind in an instant as he turned away.

Perplexed, I began to make my way to the exit. My expectations had been so high — that everyone was as happy as I was about the preacher, the church and the powerful presence of the risen Christ in that place — that I could not imagine there could be trouble. Yet there was. As a prodigal son, sadly, I had known the ugliness of the world. I had been hurt and broken by sinners in the world, but could never imagine that I would be treated the same way by someone who was supposed to be a brother to me in the church.

My feelings began to boil up, and for me that meant an extraordinary sense of disappointment. By the time I put my hand on the doorknob, and opened it to a cold,

Midwestern winter's evening, I began to sob uncontrollably. I felt as though the church and grace and new life and a new community of forgiveness and love were just all talk. The doctrines of grace were just that — doctrine, but not life. I could not stop crying. Lost within my thoughts, numbed by the cold, I did not notice my friend Sarah coming out to see me.

Sarah was the pastor's daughter. She had seen what had happened. A young wife and mother, she had been welcoming to my wife and me as we came into the congregation. As I wept just outside the fellowship hall on that frigid night, I was not aware of Sarah's presence until she patted me on the shoulder for comfort. I sought to regain my composure, but by that time it was too late. My tears were sacraments revealing a deep wound. She began to speak: 'Mike, I saw what happened. I am embarrassed and hurt for you and for us. Yes, there is a split that is causing turmoil in the church. You had no idea. This fellow who refused to shake your hand is caught up in the middle of it. I am sorry that you got caught off guard like that and that he acted so insensitively to you, especially since you had no idea what was going on.'

Then she spoke words that have stayed with me to this day and have helped others: 'Mike, don't give up on the church.'

With those simple words of gentle admonition, I lifted my head up and listened.

'As a pastor's daughter,' she said, 'I have seen this sort of thing growing up. I have seen my father and mother hurt by people in the church. Sadly, I have seen them hurt each other too. And others have hurt me as well. But the church is "on its way". We are not yet what we will be. I have come to see that I can never know forgiveness, or how to express it, without being in this place which Christ called us into called "the church". There is no life, no growth, outside of it. It is as a family of believers that we learn to live and always cling to the foot of the cross of Christ.'

That night remains one of the most important moments in my life as a believer. It was the time when I understood that we are all sinners saved by grace. We are all broken toys on the island of misfit toys, to borrow an image from an animated movie broadcast one Christmas. In this place, at this time, life and love are not perfected. We are on our way. We, who are broken, who sometimes break each other, are being put back together.

It is the grace of God in Christ, applied through the Holy Spirit breathing his Word into our souls, that is mending us.

Yet, in between brokenness and healing, we say things we shouldn't say and regret doing so. Sometimes we regret it as the words come out of our mouths, and sometimes we fail to see our need of regret and repentance for many years. Sometimes others do that to us. It is all very messy. It is all very human. It is why Christ came. One day we shall know the perfection that is promised in the Scriptures. Until then we know the process of being perfected, often on the white-hot anvil of misunderstanding and pain in our relationships. What do we do?

'Don't give up on the church.' And cling to the foot of the cross, where Jesus Christ, God incarnate, the Creator, was crucified by his own creation, where the Son's cry of 'Why?' was left unanswered by his adoring but necessarily silent Father in heaven. There, at the cross, lies all of the mystery and heartache and brokenness of the universe. Yet there, at that place 'on a hill far away', the Paschal Victim (he willingly became the sacrifice; nothing was taken from him; he freely and lovingly gave all for our sins, despite the shame) of savagery by the devil, the flesh, the world and his own friends, for our sakes, became the Paschal Victor. To be in Christ, therefore, is to follow him as we take up our crosses — sometimes crosses of being hit by friendly fire, of being wounded in the house of a friend, like Jesus — and then to kneel in total faith, complete forgiveness and wholehearted surrendering of our lives to his, and to give our burdens, and our brothers and sisters still under construction, to the one who is making us all into new people for a new household — a household of final healing.

A prayer

Grant us, O Lord of the church, living congregations in which your Spirit shall speak and work, and make me also ready to serve you in your church with the gift — even the gift of being wounded by someone in the church — that draws me closer to the cross; and grant a common life of love and grace flowing from the cross which transforms the hurt and wounds into wholeness and winsomeness, serving each other and seeking to reach the lost sheep of your flock around the world, arm in arm, broken sinners saved by grace, linked to each other and prostrate before you; through the merits and the atoning death and glorious resurrection of our King, Christ Jesus the Lord. Amen.

Acknowledgements

I wish to express my appreciation to David Woollin of Evangelical Press for his encouragement in preparing this book. Along with David, Reverend Erroll Hulse, editor of *Reformation Today*, contributed his own pastoral accounts of why this book was worth the effort. I sincerely thank you.

To the Board of Trustees of Reformed Theological Seminary, our chairman of the board, Richard Ridgeway, recently retired chairman Jim Moore, and to my friend Dr Ric Cannada, our chancellor, I send my thanks. This manuscript was worked out while I was on a sabbatical that the board graciously granted to me. The goal of this sabbatical was not to write more books! It was (and, I should say, is, as I am completing this while on that sabbatical) to be attending to healing from a serious illness. The Reverend Steve Wallace, our chief of staff and chief operating officer, my long-time friend in the ministry, also provided wisdom and encouragement to me as I recovered. They knew that, along the journey of healing, I would need a project of some kind, at just the right time, which would actually help in the process of healing.

Along with those mentioned at Reformed Theological Seminary, I thank Lyn Perez, our campus presidents and executive directors, faculty staff, staff, students, and our supporters who believe in the vision of this seminary. Without you I could not do this kind of ministry. I thank Wendy Simmons, the executive assistant to my office, for her work in editing and preparing this book, along with all the other work that she does to multiply and maximize the ministry of the gospel. Thank you, Wendy.

Finally, I wish to say how very blessed I am to have been given a wife who keeps her vows 'in sickness and in health'! As I wrote this manuscript, Mae encouraged me, prayed for me and also nursed me to health, at times even admonishing me for the sake of my health! Her unconditional love and her unceasing watchfulness will always be the first things I think of when I see this book in days to come. Thank you for showing me Christ in our marriage and encouraging me to preach the gospel in every season of life.

Now to him who is able to strengthen you according to my gospel and the preaching of Jesus Christ, according to the revelation of the mystery that was kept secret for long ages but has now been disclosed and through the prophetic writings has been made known to all nations, according to the command of the eternal God, to bring about the obedience of faith — to the only wise God be glory for evermore through Jesus Christ! Amen (Romans 16:25-27).

Notes

Preface

1. R. T. Kendall, *Total Forgiveness: Achieving God's Greatest Challenge* (London: Hodder & Stoughton, 2001).

Chapter 1 — Have you been hurt by another believer?

1. See Ken Sande, *The Peacemaker: A Biblical Guide to Resolving Personal Conflict* (Grand Rapids, Mich.: Baker Books, 3rd editon, 2004).

Chapter 2 — Interrupted by God

1. See Richard Sibbes, *The Bruised Reed* (Edinburgh: Banner of Truth Trust, 1998).

2. Robert Jamieson, A. R. Fausset and David Brown, *A Commentary, Critical and Explanatory, on the Whole Bible : With Introduction to Old Testament Literature, a Pronouncing Dictionary of Scripture Proper Names, Tables of Weights and Measures, and an Index to the Entire Bible* (Hartford, Conn.: S. S. Scranton Co., 1871). See the comment on Zechariah 13:6 and the

larger context. Available online at the Christian Classics Ethereal Library: http://www.ccel.org/ccel/jamieson/jfb.x.xxxviii.xiv.html.

Chapter 3 — When the clock stops

1. Sibbes, *The Bruised Reed.*

Chapter 4 — Take up your cross

1. From a personal conversation with Archbishop Henry Luke Orombi in 2008.

2. *The Columbia World of Quotations* (New York: Columbia University Press, 1996. www.bartleby.com/66/, accessed September 2011).

Chapter 5 — Take off your crown

1. Archibald Alexander Hodge, *The Confession of Faith; a Handbook of Christian Doctrine Expounding the Westminster Confession* (London: Banner of Truth Trust, 1958).

2. Mark Water, *The New Encyclopedia of Christian Quotations* (Grand Rapids, MI: Baker Books, 2000).

3. Gene Edwards, *Crucified by Christians* (Beaumont, TX: SeedSowers/Christian Books Pub., 1995).

4. Matthew Henry, Leslie F. Church and Gerald W. Peterman, *The NIV Matthew Henry Commentary in One Volume : Based on the Broad Oak Edition* (Grand Rapids, Mich.: Zondervan Pub. House, 1992).

5. Water, *The New Encyclopedia of Christian Quotations,* p.430.

6. Simpson, James B., comp. *Simpson's Contemporary Quotations* (Boston: Houghton Mifflin, 1988. www.bartleby.com/63/, accessed September 2011).

7. D. James Kennedy and John Blattner, *Turn it to Gold* (Ann Arbor, Mich.: Vine Books, 1991).

8. 'He's in Control', Michael Anthony Milton, *He Shall Restore* (Chattanooga, TN: Music for Missions), Compact Disc recording (© 2011 lyrics and music by Michael Milton; © 2011 Bethesda Words and Music Publishers, BMI; © 2011 recording by Music for Missions records). See http://michaelmilton.org/music.

Chapter 6 — Go to your Gethsemane

1. Frederick Brotherton Meyer, *The Secret of Guidance* (New York, NY: Fleming H. Revell Company, 1896). p.11.

2. Newman Hall, *Leaves of Healing from the Garden of Grief* (http://www.biblebb.com/quotes/quotes1104.htm, 1891).

Chapter 7 — Don't give up on the church

1. John D. Currid, *The Expectant Prophet: Habakkuk Simply Explained* (Darlington: EP Books, 2009), p.137.

2. My own testimony may be of help to someone who has been hurt and seeks healing. I refer you, humbly, to Michael A. Milton, *What God Starts God Completes: Gospel Hope for Hurting People* (Fearn, Tain, Scotland: Christian Focus Publications, 2007).

Christians expect to be troubled by the unbelieving world — but not by their brothers and sisters in the church. Unfortunately, often the case is the reverse. In this book Michael Milton brings us back to Scripture, to the experiences of Joseph and Paul, and demonstrates that it is possible to move from being a victim to being a victor, even when Christian bonds make the wounds all the deeper. Full of personal and pastoral wisdom, this little book will help many believers face a trauma all too common in the Christian church, yet all too seldom addressed in the literature.

Iain D. Campbell, Free Church of Scotland, Isle of Lewis

I wish that this excellent, practical, healing book had been published years ago. I would have used many copies to lift up those severely wounded in the house of friends. Highly commended.

Erroll Hulse, Editor of *Reformation Today*

I wish this book did not need to be written, but it does, because far too many Christians are wounded every year by fellow believers. As a 'spiritual medic', Mike has treated these wounds for years. His counsel is insightful, compassionate and solidly biblical; it will help to heal many wounded saints.

Ken Sande, President, Peacemaker˚ Ministries